Battles in the Pacific World War II

My Personal War Causing PTSD

by
Frank S. Wright

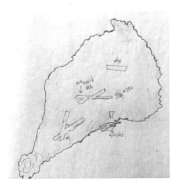

Dorrance Publishing Co
585 Alpha Drive
Suite 103
Pittsburgh, PA 15238
Visit our website at *www.dorrancebookstore.com*

ISBN: 978-1-6442-6949-7
eISBN: 978-1-6442-6302-0

Battles in the Pacific World War II

My Personal War Causing PTSD

by

Frank S. Wright

DORRANCE
PUBLISHING CO
EST. 1920
PITTSBURGH, PENNSYLVANIA 15238

I fought like mad as the Japanese stormed down the hill yelling "Malians you die, Malians you die!" I emptied my rifle magazine twice. Out of ammo, I slashed and plunged my bayonet into as many as I could until...

Foreword

I think I know why and how I ended up with PTSD. The "why" is that you are scared—shaking scared. It remains in your memory and you recall those instances. A tough marine usually does not admit they are scared. Now the "how" is another story, and here is mine.

It started with my enlistment in the U.S. Marine Corps back in 1942. 76 *years ago*. I was A boy of sixteen who was still a very young child with a mind of adventure and very easy to impress. A boy whose brain was easy to invade and easy to train the way the military could use.

On December 7, 1941, the Japanese bombed Pearl Harbor, and the U.S. President, Franklin D. Roosevelt, reported to the U.S. Congress and said, "We are in a state of war." I was very busy that Sunday in December, sitting at our kitchen table making balsa wood airplanes. The plane was a Forker D-8. Woolworth—a Little Rock, Arkansas, Five and Ten department store—wanted that plane for display in their toy section. They were giving me an airplane *free* for my work. My mind was filled with pictures of war and airplanes of that time. So two weeks after the Pearl Harbor bombing, I went to the recruiting office of the marine corps in Little Rock to join-up. The marines, navy, and army would not take you in unless you were seventeen and weighed at least 130 pounds. I was only sixteen and would not be seventeen until July 5, 1942. I did not weigh the required amount. So now I would be on my first travel of lying and deceit. I just had to help protect our country.

I bought five pounds of bananas and some other things to get the weight restriction taken care of. I talked like mad to get my mother and dad sold on the idea of me becoming a marine. I guess I sold them on the idea after I told them about the $10,000 insurance I would have if I was able to join-up. But—and it was a big but—was that I did not have a birth certificate. Somehow that was overlooked due to my being born at home or someplace else in Arkansas. They said they would get a delayed birth certificate that indicated that I was born on December 5, 1924, which would make me seventeen, and if I could meet all other rules and regulations, I could join the marines.

I went to the marine recruiting office in Little Rock to join the marines, and they told me I would have to wait until they had at least eight more people join in order to have a squad for the trip by train to San Diego, California. Finally, on January 21, 1942, I was called to sign the papers and take a physical. Well, my fake birth certificate worked. My weight was just fine. The recruiting sergeant said he had changed the rules to allow my weight of 128 pounds to pass.

So I signed up for four years in order to get into the marine air wing as an airplane mechanic (he said). Here we were, nine fighting marine corps recruits with a new squad leader, Private C. W. White in control of our recruit papers, headed for San Diego Marine Corps Recruit Depot. There were no airplanes anywhere near this place for us to learn mechanics with, and the first person to meet us at the train *was the devil himself, my drill instructor,* with his two assistants.

SGT. H.L. ALLEN, HEAD DRILL INSTRUCTOR
CORP. R. RYCE, DRILL INSTRUCTOR ASSISTANT
CORP. S. C. ALEXANDER, DRILL INSTRUCTOR ASSISTANT
150th PLATOON, USMC, SAN DIEGO, CA. January 1942
(U.S. MARINE CORPS — FIRST TO FIGHT)

1942

Boot Camp

16 years old, 1942, Boot Camp picture —Frank Wright

The first thing they gave me was a gas masks. Now that was a wake-up call. I had not even thought of that kind of war. Where were my Blues? In all the movies, I had seen the marines wearing those great looking Blues. Then those *green*-colored shorts. (It turned out that I would wear the green-colored shorts for the next five years; I really liked them). Over-sized field shoes, over-sized trousers (girls wore pants), and a green blouse (I thought girls wore these things). I got a package of double-edged razor blades and a razor. I had never shaved and didn't know how. However, the D.I. said, "You will shave every day, if you need it or not." So I did. We were issued a sea bag and were told to put all our gear in it as we were issued it. We were issued a rifle from the World War I era. A bolt-action Springfield Model 03, covered in cosmoline. We were taught how to clean those rifles many times. We were taught how to fire the bolt-operated rifle quickly. We did not fire the Springfield 03 for our record, as we were going to be issued a new rifle called a Garand M1 (gas-operated, magazine-fed, eight rounds loaded). We were taught how to shoot, where to shoot, and what to shoot at. We were taught to *kill* or be killed. I shot a high score on the rifle range and was an expert rifle shooter and a 45-cal. expert pistol shooter. In other words, I was good. We were taught how to use the bayonet and where to stick the enemy in order to *kill* them quickly. We were taught Judo, the art of self-defense, and how to *kill* the enemy with one blow. We marched, marched, marched, marched. We were taught everything a marine should know in just eight weeks. We were hit, poked, and pushed. We sang a song under a bucket as a punishment for calling the rifle a gun: *This is my rifle, this is my gun (holding my crotch). My rifle is to shoot, and my gun is for fun.* And if you dropped the rifle, you usually slept with it for a week. We were called every name in the book, and some they won't even print. My boot-camp training was the hardest and most intense training and experience of my entire life. I had never had any person call me those names; they treated me like I was a non-person. They loved me and trained me hard and made a man of me. I still think of them even after over ninety years. This type of training has saved my life many times.

I graduated from boot camp on March 19, 1942, feeling like I really was a marine. I came into boot training on January 21, 1942 an innocent little 128 pound, 5-foot six-and-a-half "child." Not seventeen for six more months. I left boot camp as a 150 pound, 5-foot, 7-inche Marine. I reported to duty at the Naval Air Station, Tongue Point, Oregon, on March 21, 1942, posted as guard duty The only airplanes here were PBY Seaplanes and there was no schooling scheduled for training. We were to guard the Tongue Point Naval Yard mountain overlooking the Columbia River, the entrance to the Pacific Ocean. Also, it overlooked the route of the new Kaiser ships on the way to Astoria, Oregon

Port Docks that were to be loaded for oversea duties. This little mountain was also used for the storing of ammunition that would be shipped overseas.

Astoria, Oregon was a few miles up the Columbia River from the bar (entrance) to the Pacific Ocean. The Columbia River entrance was also a gateway to Portland, Oregon; Longview, Washington; and Seattle, Washington. The navy and marines at Tongue Point, as well as the army at Fort Stevens and a naval attachment at Longview, were the security for that river. Fort Stevens Army Installation was security at the entrance of the Columbia River in Hammond, Oregon. Fort Stevens military installation guarded the mouth of the Columbia River. It was the primary military defense installation in the three-fort harbor defense system, along with Forts Canby and Columbia in Washington. Fort Stevens was built near the end of the American Civil War. On the night of June 21st–22nd 1942, the Japanese submarine I-25 surfaced just off Fort Stevens and fired seventeen shells from her deck gun. Actually, she made history by being the only military installation in the continental United States to come under enemy fire in World War II. This Japanese submarine did no damage to the fort itself but did destroy the fort's backstop at their baseball field. The Ellwood Oil Field near Santa Barbara, California, had really been shelled earlier by submarine, but that was not a military post. The Japanese I-25 had a crew of ninety-seven and had entered the US coastal waters by following our fishing boats to avoid the mine fields in the area. The fort's commander ordered an immediate blackout and refused to permit his men to return fire, as this would have revealed their position. Some of the submarine's shells severed several large telephone cables and also landed near the concrete pillboxes.

One thing this attack did do was help create the 1942 West Coast Invasion scare. Rolls of barbed wire were strung from Point Adams southward in case of invasion. I really was very upset at the possibility that this was "it." We were going to be right in the middle of a shooting war. I felt the population of Oregon and Washington were not fully prepared for any kind of occupation. The possibility of invasion along the Oregon coast, and even the mouth of the Columbia River, had given the harbor defense system an encouragement to better fortify the area. It also kind of changed my mind as to what part I would play in an enemy invasion—something a sixteen-year-old boy should not be thinking about.

About two weeks later, I met a really nice girl in Astoria and talked to her about the shelling at Fort Stevens. It had not made an impression on her and did not seem to bother her. I guess the population in Astoria had not thought of it as dangerous. I tried to date her, Bernice Salmon, and get to know her better. She told me she was going steady with a marine at Tongue Point, but she had a younger sister, Katherine Salmon, who would be coming into town the following week. I thought it would be nice if we could double-date at that time. So she and her date and me and my date Katherine all went to a movie in town. After the movie, we escorted the girls back to their apartment, and we went back to our barracks. I really liked Katherine: young, long blonde hair, and a little timid. She was still in high school and 14 (almost 15) years old.

Well, I was sixteen, remember. We had all decided to meet the next weekend and have a picnic at the local town park. The park had a public swimming pool and a nice place for a picnic as well. Katherine would come with her friend LaVelle. I would bring a friend, Private Bill Redburn, for her. The older sister, Bernice Salmon, would be with her date, PFC Lloyd Heini. We took the bus over to the park, had a good swim, and got dressed. The three marines were in their marine blues and really looked outstanding. Of course we wanted to look our best. The three girls really looked really nice in their swimsuits and really looked nice in their street clothes. While we were eating and visiting, I found out that Katherine and LaVelle were going to Westport High School and lived in Woodson, Oregon. Bernice was out of school and working in Astoria. Then we heard about the suspected Japanese SPY network in Woodson Hills, just about half a mile from their home in Woodson. The day before the Pearl Harbor attack, the entire population of J population of Japanese alleged spies disappeared. The Japanese, and also a German radio operator, had left the country. The younger children of the spies had been going to school with Katherine and her younger sister Eileen, and they were gone as well. It turned out that the Japanese camp and homes overlooked the Columbia River, which was the shipping route from Kaiser Shipping Yards in Portland. Newly constructed naval vessels, including aircraft carriers, would come down the Columbia to port docks in Astoria, get supplied, and then go out into the ocean. Squadron after squadron of aircraft would fly over Katherine's house and land on the small

carriers stationed in the ocean. The alleged German short-wave radio operative could relay the messages of all the traffic going up and down the Columbia. Boy, that was really some news. Imagine, my "girlfriend" was living near an alleged Japanese spy encampment. Katherine, her brother and two sisters with their friends, had even gone up to the Jap camp and had a picnic in front of the tunnel that had been constructed. She had told us of the time she and some of the school kids had gone up to the camp (after they had moved out) and saw all kinds of Japanese papers, cards, and different things at their camp. The Japanese had been working at the tunnel and tending the railroad tracks leading to the tunnel. They were using the tunnel for transportation to the log dump on the other side of the mountain. This was mostly the Kerry Log Line for the mountain timber. Before the Japanese moved out and before the Pearl Harbor attack, someone proceeded to blow up the cave entrance. Were they saboteurs or just someone covering up something to store and retrieve later?

I saw Katherine one more time when I traveled to Portland with four other marines that had the weekend off. We were going up the Columbia River highway and would be traveling past her family's farm. I asked the driver of our group to go down the dike road that led past her home. She was not at her house, but her mother indicated she was out in the hay field helping her father make hay. I say "indicated," as her mother did not speak English very well. Her mother and father were of Finnish descent, along with all their children. Her mother had not picked up the English language as well as their father and children. The children spoke Finn to their mother and English to their father. Their mother had been born in Finland and the father and children were born in the United States. Katherine was riding on the mower, and her father was driving. Katherine had a bandana tired around her pretty blonde hair and two red bandanas tide together around her chest area for a halter. She was very embarrassed at my dropping in on her. After a few words, saying I was sorry about our meeting on the street that time, I had to leave and get back to camp. I thought she was neat-looking sitting on the tractor mower.

Katherine and I didn't see each other after our picnic party. She was busy helping on the family farm during the summer. She was in a family of nine children; the four boys were in the military, and three of the girls were away from home working, leaving her younger sister and her to help out with the cows and farm work. We did correspond by mail several times and kept in contact with each other. Most of our guard duties changed, and we did not get off as often as before the submarine fiasco. We did meet one time when we had a lack of information in our correspondence. She said she would not be coming in to Astoria that weekend, and I said I didn't think I could get liberty. Well, I got off duty, and I went into town. I met a girl near the USO, and we were going to the USO dance. I was walking with her on the way to the dance and met Katherine on the street. She was able to get into town, and I was able to get off duty. Well, to put it this way—I still hear about it.

It was on about July 17, 1942 when I received orders, along with eight other marines, to prepare for an assignment to a special gunnery school in Port Angeles, Washington. It would probably be for two weeks, and then we would return to Tongue Point for further assignment. I dropped a quick line to Katherine explaining that I was sorry about the street meeting and that I would be leaving the area for a few weeks. I didn't say where, as I thought it would be secretive information. I just hoped she would believe me this time, as I had problems before when I said I could not get off on liberty.

We got in Port Angeles and got more information as to why we were getting this gunnery schooling. We were going to be trained in the operation of the 20-mm Oerlikon machine gun at the anti-aircraft training center. The first week would be tearing it down and putting it back together. The second week we would be firing the anti-aircraft at a sock being pulled by an airplane. Jokingly he said that if we hit the plane and knocked it down, we would have to pay for it. We were taught how to judge the airplane's speed, length, and how high it was flying. These 20-mm guns were normally installed on ships for protection against the attack of airplanes. I was thinking at the time that it would be just the thing to have them all over the Tongue Point Naval Station for protection from airplanes and other invasion vehicles. Maybe this is what the harbor defense system had in mind—to install them all around Tongue Point, Fort Stevens, Fort Camby, and Fort Columbia. After our two weeks of training, our scores were posted. I found on my record files that on July 28, 1942, my score was 3.55. I guess it was okay, as we shot at the sock 5 times. So 3.55 out of 5 wasn't too bad.

I was now seventeen years old on July 5, 1942 and had been promoted to PFC. I was earning $28 a month—$5 extra as an expert rifleman and $1 extra for being expert pistol. That was the largest amount of money I had ever made in my life.

When I got back to Tongue Point, I found that quite a few of the marines on our guard duty assignment had been transferred out. They had been sent to 3rd Base Depot, Destination FMFTC, Camp Elliot, San Diego, California. They were to be transferred as replacements to wherever. We were left at Tongue Point with half a crew and had to do double guard-duty. Before the replacement came, we had been doing eight hours on and eight hours off. Now we were to do four hours on and four hours off. I pulled that duty for a couple weeks, and it really was tough (not enough sleep). Then one night

I could hear the sound of the one-cylinder fishing boats over the pounding of the rain. I was wearing my guard-duty greens, field boots, overcoat, rain poncho, gas masks, ammunition belt full of ammo, M-1 rifle, and steel helmet. Walking guard up the dark dirt road on Post 3, I met the guard on Post 2. We reported all was well on both posts and started down the dirt road to post 1. I came around the corner, slipped, and fell down the cliff. I fell about ten feet, flat on my stomach. There was one rock, or boulder and I fell face down, and that boulder went between my legs, and it *really hurt*. I was out like a light and unable to walk. When I did not report to Post 1 as scheduled, he called the corporal of the guard. Of course, everybody thought the Japanese or one of the few saboteurs we had heard about had gotten me, They found me at the bottom of the cliff and said I looked like a stack of military equipment soaked in mud and rain. They transported me to the base hospital, and I was in the hospital for thirty-one days, at least until the swelling went down so I could walk again. While I was in the hospital, an additional group of marines were transferred in for guard duty, and the shifts were back to regular hours. But I really did not like the idea of guard duty and was looking for a time I could transfer out to another duty.

The time came. In October 1942, a marine staff sergeant from headquarters camp, Pendleton, California, came to Tongue Point looking for volunteers for the Special Forces of the 4th Marine Raiders Battalion. These Raiders would be commanded by Major James Roosevelt. Major James Roosevelt was the son of our president, Franklin D. Roosevelt. Now what danger could it be if the president's son was going to lead us? So I asked if I could be interviewed. When they saw that I was a determined to fight the enemy when asked to, they asked me if I was determined to *kill* and if it bothered me. I told them I could *kill* and I would *kill* if I was ordered to. They looked at my marksmanship with the rifle, pistol, bayonet, 20 mm anti-aircraft, and Judo. After several more questions, they said to watch the transfer board early the next day.

On October 28, 1942, PFC Frank S. Wright was transferred to Base Depot A, San Diego, California, FMFTC. On October 30, 1942, PFC Wright joined 3rd Base Depot, Detached FMFTC, Camp Elliot, San Diego, California, with First Sergeant Elmer J. Phenix. On November 20, 1942, Captain Alvis H. Allen was in charge. Then, on November 23, 1942, PFC Frank S. Wright joined Co. D, 4th Marine Raider Bn. Camp Pendleton with 1st. Lieutenant William L. Flake, USMC Company Commander. I was to help form the 4th Marine Raiders with Major James Roosevelt Battalion Commander.

I was now a squad leader in the first ever Special Forces of the United States Marine Corps. The Marine Corps now had the 1st, 2nd, 3rd and 4th Battalion Raiders (Special Forces). They were to be the first to fight and would be trained to be experts in night-fighting and hitting the enemy silently. We trained on the 122,000-acre military reservation at Camp Pendleton, California.

Every officer and enlisted man was hand-picked from volunteers. All had already undergone the preliminary rigors of the regular marine training. We had been issued the K-Bar knife, twelve inches overall in length , with a six-and-a-half-inch single blade, three-quarters of an inch wide. We were also issued a Marine Raider Stiletto. The Marine Stiletto was the first official knife designed by a marine corps officer. This knife was twelve-inches long and a seven-inch blade sharpened on both sides and a needle point, actually designed for night-fighting and silent *kills*.

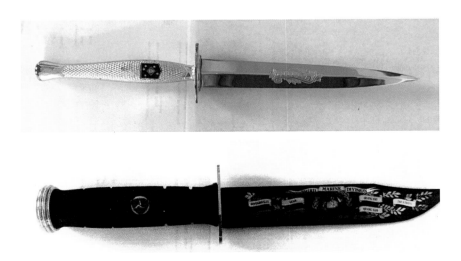

General James Roosevelt and I

Training in the Raiders was far more intense than the regular boot camp training. Everything that the enlisted man did, so did the officers. The officers ate the same food, wore the same clothes, and slept in the same area. When we went on a hike for forty-two miles, fifteen miles, or ten miles, we would find our officers right along beside us. I have walked five feet away from our commander on those long hikes. He was a great marine and became a good friend during my Raider career and after the war.

Later on I wanted to get letters from home and from my girlfriend, so I wrote her and brought her up to date on some of my activity in the Raiders. I also wrote to my mother to give my family in Arkansas the news about being in the same outfit as Roosevelt's son. Letters from home were a big thing for us in the military. The military thought this was very important as well. We would get mail from family even during combat in the Raiders. When we wrote home while in a combat zone, all we had to do was write FREE on the envelope, and off it went. However, it had to go through one of the officers first to ensure we did not tell any military secrets.

1943

Finally we had completed our Marine Raider training and received our orders to ship out for combat in the Pacific Theater. Our 4th Raiders had designed and formatted the training that would continue for all marines going through combat training at Camp Pendleton. The training area was officially designated Raider Replacement Training Company, and later the Training Center. We embarked aboard the USS President Polk (APA -103) at San Diego, California, February 5, 1943. The USS President Polk was a converted luxury liner and still had most of the state rooms and banquet rooms aboard. The officers got the state rooms (for planning the operation, of course) and the rest of us got the crew's mess hall and quarters with the upper and lower poop deck. The head (toilets) were converted little sheds attached to the port and starboard sides. The heads had fifteen seats and a water valley under the seats that was pumped with fresh ocean water running under the seats. Of course, you always wanted to sit on the middle seat so you would not get splashed on as the ship went up and down. We did our exercise on the top deck every morning and had church services there as well. When the weather got warmer, most of the marines slept on the top deck in our sleeping roll. We were reminded and told that two men caught in the same bed roll get a court martial, discharged, and sent home—period.

We passed over the equator on February 16, 1943. A celestial equator is an imaginary line drawn around the earth equally distant from both poles, dividing the earth into northern and southern hemispheres and constituting the parallel of latitude 0 degrees; it is also referred to as the International Date Line. The navy always have celebrations each time their ship reached that area for the pollywogs (new people) that had never been there before. That is a secret type of celebration and cannot be discussed here. It celebrates King Neptune and his family. It is called "The Shell-back Ceremony."

We finally saw land on March 1, 1943, and the marines who were really "land-lovers" were really happy, as we had a few days on the voyage of rough waters. We arrived at dock on Espiritu Santo Island, New Hebrides Islands, and made ready to disembark. We needed a prayer of thanks. Our Raider Padre was Father Paul J. Redmond and was dearly loved by all Raiders. He had given services to all denominations during our training and onboard our ship. He had endured the hard training with the Raiders and given us spiritual support from the first day back in Camp Pendleton. We asked him for a "thank you" prayer before we debarked ship. Also, we asked him to talk to Colonel James Roosevelt, our battalion commander, and asked him to relay a message to the Polk's ship's captain and keep him busy for a little bit. In other words, keep him occupied and off of the main deck.

On the last night aboard the Polk, several Raiders from company 4AN and 4Q got together with 2nd Lieutenant Thomas J. Conner, 4AN Weston A. Hartman, Sergeant Stanley Kondracki, and Gunner Louis L. Barnhart of the motor transport. This was the start of "The Story of the Missing Piano."

Lieutenant Conner would get the O.D. deck officer to go to forward with him to check on the problem they were having at the forward hatch. When the coast was clear, a rather large covered object was rolled across the deck to the gang way. A smaller LCVP (landing /craft /vehicle /personnel) approached the gangway and the "PIANO" was offloaded aboard and headed to the beach. All the Padre had said was, "It would be nice to have a piano for Mass." So what the Padre wanted, the Raiders provided. Cpl. Harold Hart and myself from the 4DQ had about thirty-two men waiting for the piano. A truck had been provided for by a gunnery sergeant from the motor transport. This large object was loaded and guarded by the 4th Raiders. Our company commander, Captain Donald S. Floyd, was in the ship's bay with an ear infection at the time and knew nothing of the affair. He could not understand why we were being called "Roosevelt and his Thousand Thieves."

Father Redmond said he had seen a large object being pushed across the main deck and placed in a large boat docked near the gangplank. He said he had expressed his concern and told the robbers not to tell him where it was to be delivered, in case he was ever asked where it was.

Me, and my squad, and three squads from company 4AN, delivered the piano to the area where the native church was located. We put the piano in the church and covered with a nicer looking canvas. Several days later, the ship's captain demanded that the piano be returned or that he would report the theft to Washington. Colonel Roosevelt and the ship's captain had asked the Padre if he knew where it was and responded with the truth, as not knowing where it was. Not knowing, he had been saying Mass at the native church with his music and other sermon material on the bulky object just the size of an altar. So the piano was returned, and all was well between Father Redmond and Colonel Roosevelt.

In the meantime, the 3rd Raiders had bad-mouthed the 4th Raiders for doing such a dastardly deed. How could the dirty bastards do such a thing? Later, when the 3rd Raiders combat gear was being unloaded on the descending cargo nets, they found that with the combat was the ship's washing machines. Then the 3rd Raiders were also called "Harry the Horse and his 1,000 thieves," like those of Roosevelt's thieves.

It felt good to have solid land under my feet, but things seem to be a little mixed up around the area that they had assigned us. It was one of those "hurry up and wait" routines. it seemed to me that they did not know just what area we were going to be assigned.

We were assigned a tent camp that had already been put together, even with a dirt road winding through the tents. We had eight Raiders to the tent with the sides rolled up. The rain ditches were already dug around the tent. After we had our assigned tent, unpacked our bedding from our pack roll we got the word to fall in for further instructions. We were then told not to get too settled, as we may be moved to another area. It seemed we may either be sent out on mission or some kind of organizational change. The word came down later that on March 15, 1942 we would be the 1st Marine Raider Regiment and composed of H&S Company, 1st, 2nd, 3rd and 4th Marine Raider Battalions. Then, on March 22, 1942, our Battalion, the 4th, would be changed to 4th Marine Raider Battalion, 1st Marine Raider Regiment, 1st Marine Amphibious Corps. E Company would be disbanded, and then two days later on the 25th, A Company would be N Company, B Company would be O Company and C was designated as P Company, and then P Company would be Q Company. Boy, what a shake-up. It finally was all organized, and most of us knew what outfit we were in and what camp we were going to be in. I was now in Q Company and would be staying in the first camp we had originally been put in. We were told that Major James Roosevelt was now headed back to the States. He had a case of malaria and other things that he had gotten on his first campaign with the Raiders on Makin. Our new battalion commander would be Major James R. Clark. He came aboard on April 29, 1943. Major Clark would be our battalion commander until May 4, 1943, and at that time Lieutenant Colonel Michael S. Currin would take over.

We were in training to work in dense jungle and with fast travel without sound. We all felt something was up, as we were doing things a little different than before. Sure enough, we got the word that we would be shipping out right away. We did not know where or when, but were ordered to pack our sea bags secure , and our personal pack should contain things to live out of if necessary.

On May 31, 1943, Q Company got the word, and we were to board the USS Penn (APA-25) and arrive at Tetere, Guadalcanal, BSI on June 2, 1943. We were to participate in patrol duty and wipe out organized enemy position. We were told not to get comfortable with where we will be billeted. On June 20, 1943, O Company embarked aboard the USS Dent (APD-9), and P Company embarked aboard the USS Waters (APD-8) and headed to Tetere Guadalcanal to meet up with our Q Company.

While on patrol duty on Guadalcanal after we arrived, I got hit with either Malaria or Dengue, or Cat Fever as some had called it. I really had a high fever and sore body parts and shakes. Female mosquitoes were known to carry the fever around camp on Guadalcanal. There was Bad muddy waters, marshes, frogs in the millions, and animal poop in about every piece of water.

When the three companies got together on Guadalcanal, we headed for New Georgia on June 21, 1943. I heard our company was leaving, so I snuck out of the First Aid Tent without the release of our corpsman. I couldn't see my squad going in combat without me, as I heard it was going to be rough. Besides, we were to carry the Boy's 55-caliber Anti-Tank Rifle on our next encounter. The Boy's 55-caliber rifle weighed 35 pounds, and the ammunition weighed about the same. There was going to be a lot of walking through the jungle. The first time, we landed where we met up with enemy fire. That was really scary for me. These guys were firing back and did not want us to land. Later I found out that it was a small unit that we had encountered, and we dispatched them pretty quickly. The main body of the 1st and 4th Raiders cleared Enogai Inlet, which was about 4,000 yards along the coast. I had been set up along a trail with my squad and the .55-caliber Boy's Anti-Tank Rifle to protect from any surprise that may be waiting for us, like a tank or pillboxes. The 60-mm mortar squad and their small-weapons squad had advanced closer in on the jungle. At daybreak, J. J. Johnson (of Mississippi) 4th DQ and the mortar squad, along with some of the 1st Raiders, had Japanese in front, in the back, and in the middle, and the Japanese were trying to regroup and pulled in behind the Raiders. For whatever the reason or the cause, the Raiders were pinned down. There were Japanese snipers everywhere in the trees. I was in a fire fight on the trail when I heard all hell break out in the jungle area. Our squad hightailed it over to give assistance and got in the middle of all the ruckus. It had been decided that the mortars could be used to clear the overhead mass where the snipers were. All the "tommy-guns" were good for was to just spray the trees where we thought the snipers were. Johnson's squad would run to a clearing and lay down a heavy fire directed toward the overhead trees, jungle vines, and whatever laid in the distance. As they busied themselves manning their mortars, the overhead Japanese snipers had a field day firing all around them. Johnson told me later, when I was the executive secretary, editor and publisher of *The Raider Patch* for the Marine Raider Association that he lost a lot of good men on that ambush. Johnson said that PFC David "Stud" Van Fleet (Kingsville, Texas) felt a slug zip under his rear end, and he quickly took his helmet off his head and put it over his rear end. He must have thought the sniper's rifle sites were off or their marksmanship was just bad. He said that Jack Salters, (Del Rio, Tx.) 4th DQ, who was standing about twenty feet to my left, took a hit from a shell when it exploded in front of him. Jack took a shrapnel in his leg but was still able to continue firing. He missed the rest of the war with that wound. We had to dig foxholes where we were as deep as we could make them, with roots sticking our ribs to help keep us awake. Sounds of wounded Raiders could be heard throughout the night, and some did not make it through the night. These sounds were next to ours, or just in front of ours. Some were Japs begging for help pretending to be marines. Johnson said that Private Gerald Ayers, Private Donald Barnes, and Private First Class Walter Gibbins, all of 4DQ, were killed attempting to rescue each other. This was brotherly love, sacrifice, and bravery. I did not know them but did know how it could have happened. Those three could have been replacements and did not know their trickery. I found out later, according to Assistant Chief of Staff, Headquarters, U.S. Marine Corps, that the 1st and 4th Raider Battalions had come head-to-head with the enemy that occupied very strong positions, heavily covered with coral and well camouflaged, with twenty to thirty machine guns. Heavy machine-gun positions were covered by riflemen in the trees. As the thick jungle canopy prohibited the use of our light mortars, Colonel Liversedge ordered a withdrawal toward Enogai Point with the 1st Raider Battalion covering.

At 1100 the next day (21 July 1943), the 4th and 1st disengaged and moved back to Enogai. All wounded and dead were evacuated, and all weapons and ammunitions were salvaged. We had been in this area of New Georgia for two days and really got a taste of one-on-one battle. I tell you for a fact that I was really scared. I felt like a human target. The yelling at night made you want to help when you knew you couldn't. I think of that time to this day and night.

We stayed there at Draqon Peninsula at Enogai, New Georgia for patrols and mop-up until August 28, 1943. We then embarked aboard the USS McKean (APD-5) and the USS Waters (APD-8) at Enogai, New Georgia, and debarked at Tetere Point, Guadalcanal, on August 30, l943

On September 4, 1943, we embarked aboard the USS American Legion (APD-17) at Tetere Point, Guadalcanal and arrived at Noumea, New Caledonia on September 8, 1943. We were camped at Camp Allard at the Mission St. Louis. I tell you for a fact that I was ready for a good rest. I had been on so many navy ships, I must have thought I was part of the navy.

I had been shaking from malaria most of the time and from being scared most of the time I had snuck out from the field hospital before I was considered well. You use your training, and most of the time you stay safe. Most of the time now was routine marine training and eating. I was really ready for real food. I had lost a lot of weight, cut from vines, twigs, coral and blisters. We then heard that the first echelon of our battalion was going to Auckland, New Zealand. The ships were going to New Zealand for repairs and scraping of barnacles from the ships' hulls. It would take about two weeks for their repairs, and the Raiders were to go along as passengers for rest and rehabilitation. On October 1, l943, all of the first echelon ran around camp with smiles on their faces and embarked aboard the SS. Mormac Port, at Noumea, New Caledonia for a cruise to a friendly island. They arrived at Auckland, New Zealand on October 3, 1943 for rest and *rehabilitation*. They were really ready for that rest part. Both sections that were to leave for Auckland had been told to clean up and really look the part as well-dressed Marines. Most of us had our liberty greens in the bottom of our sea bags. We dug them out and pressed them under our mattresses, along with our khaki shirts and field scarfs (ties). We shined our dress shoes as well, which were also on the bottoms of our sea bags.

The first section orders were to stay in New Zealand for about two weeks, and we in the second section had more time to prepare ourselves. The first section arrived back in Tetera, Guadalcanal on October 19, 1943 aboard the USS Tryon. The second section had already left aboard the USS Rixey on October 18, 1943. We arrived in New Zealand on October 21, 1943. It would have been nice to have been given a heads up as to what to expect when we arrived. When we arrived on the 21st of October, we were billeted near a camp that had previously been occupied by the New Zealand Army, who would be coming back home from their training exercises or combat operation. It seems the Raiders from the first section had been dating the New Zealand Army's girlfriends and wives while they were away on operations elsewhere. When we arrived, the New Zealand guys were really upset. When we went on our first liberty on October 22, 1943, we met the New Zealand guys on Queen Street, which is the main street going through Auckland. The shore patrol and M.P.'s had a field day breaking up all the "discussions" the two groups were having. After that, it was called "The Queen Street War." It was not a good sight on either side, but especially on our side, as we were the visiting personnel in their country. New Zealand is a beautiful country, and I would have liked to visit Auckland again after the war. I had met several people in the farmland surrounding Auckland. I had met one girl and her family that I thought had an unusual name. The girl's name was Joyce Horsepool. For some reason, I don't remember the other family's name. I had met another girl in downtown Auckland with an unusual name also. Her name was "Mazie Philpott." She was a singer in one of the nice establishments on Queen Street.

The second section was lucky as the shipyards were getting overloaded with repair work and the ships were getting backed up on the docks. This backup made a delay in our return to our base in the 'Canal.

We left aboard the Australian USAT Maui on November 17, 1943 and arrived at the 'Canal on November 20, 1943. We had been gone almost a month on our two-week rehab trip. We had been able to tour the countryside and take in a lot of scenery around Auckland.

However, somewhere along my tour of the Pacific, I got the malaria bug again. The shakes and chills were harder to shake this time. I was transferred from the ship's hospital to the one in Tassafaronga, as they thought they would lose me if I didn't take my medicine correctly. I was finally discharged from the hospital in Tassafaronga, Guadalcanal on December 24, 1943; Christmas Eve in the tropics. I did not go to my old Company DQ of the Raiders. I was told Major Robert H. Thomas had been the commander of the 4th Marine Raider Battalion since September 15, 1943, just before we started our New Zealand "tours." The Raiders were now renamed the 4th Marines into the division units and were being broken up. I would be transferred to the replacement battalion on Guadalcanal. So I spent Christmas Day, 1943 with guys I had never seen before. I stayed in the replacement battalion just waiting for a transfer. I did do some searching around the jungle looking for holdout Japanese not turning themselves in or giving up. Taking lone patrols was frowned upon, however. We had organized patrols in the daytime and got a few that would not surrender. I kind of got a nickname and was referred to as BoonDocker and a lone hunter. I am not proud of that part, but it was a time in my life that still bugs me. I know I was really scared some of those times.

1944

On February 1, 1944, the Raiders were now called the 2nd Battalion, 4th Marines. On January 21, 1944, I was finally transferred to Co. K, 3rd Battalion, 21st Marines, 3rd Marine Division as squad leader. I was then transferred over to the H & S Company, Weapons 21st Marines. I was to be the Weapons Platoon, H&S Company, 21st Marines, 3rd Division, on the next campaign. So training started with the new company, new leaders, and new weapons. We knew just lying around did not set well with our commanders. It showed up in their training schedule and their voices. It got more serious during the first part of June 1944, and we had to start training earlier in the mornings, getting into a Higgins boat on shore, going out to a destroyer or troop ship, and climbing up the rope ladders. Rough seas, calm seas, it didn't matter. Then one day our "June in the tropics" came to a halt. On June 3, 1944, we boarded the USS Rixey and headed for Guam, in the Marianas. We, the 3rd Marine Division, were chosen to recapture it from the Japanese. The Japanese had captured Saipan, Tinian, and Guam in 1941. In history this will be called "The Second War for Guam." One thing that happened seemed odd at first but made since after we heard the reason for the change. We were told to change all of our paper money we had in our possession into what they call "Hawaii Dollars." The "Hawaii Dollars" were of $1, $5, $10, and $20 American denominations, but the difference was they had "Hawaii" printed in large letters across the faces of the bills. Anyone caught with a bill without the large "Hawaii" print on it would have to give it to the government and be questioned by the military as to the source of the bill. The Hawaii bill was the only legal tender in the Pacific Theater. Now for the reason: It seems that when the Japanese occupied Guam, Tinian, and Saipan in 1941, they also captured the military personnel and *The Military Paymaster*. At the military headquarters, the Japanese took possession of all American monies and all of the island's American money. Therefore, when the American Forces re-occupied the Marianas, our military did not want *any* Marine to obtain possession of all or any of this loot and send it home. So all mail during and way after the operation would be censored. When you get your sea bag back with all of your gear, you should exchange that also. You could not spend *any* money without the print "Hawaii" on it.

On June 5, 1944 the invasion force of 2nd and 3rd Division left Guadalcanal and sailed to Saipan, Tinian, and Guam. The 2nd Division was to re-take Saipan and Tinian. The 3rd Division was to be the floating reserve for the 2nd. Saipan was not supposed to be a real long battle to secure it; then they would go on over and finish off Tinian. It took three weeks and three days to secure and control. Part of the 2nd Division crossed over to Tinian and got that island secured and kept a watch to keep them from going over to Guam.

While waiting for our word to attack, we had the most interesting visual of the biggest aircraft dog fight in history. The military historians dub this "The Great Mariana's Turkey Shoot," where the U.S. decimated the Japanese carrier task force, sinking three carriers and shooting down 330 of the 430 planes launched. We were sitting aboard the ship watching all this on June 19, 1944. I have dreamed of this many, many times, as I had long ago dreamed of doing air battles while building airplanes. But this was real, and people were dying.

The Fox Company, 21st Marines, 3rd Division landed on July 21, 1944 at Agat beach area near Mt. Alifan. When we landed, the area had been bombarded so much that the town of Agat was almost destroyed. There were 900 airplanes and all of the invasion ships blasting the shoreline where we were to land. Several tiny rocket-launcher vessels floated near the island just above the coral reefs and blasted unmercifully just before we landed. When we landed, we had very little opposition except for a few mortar attacks. I saw one water buffalo standing in the water-filled area feeding, as if it was an everyday happening. The buffalo did not get wounded during the complete shelling. We passed by, and it didn't leave his feeding area. We were fighting on clear ground and low brush and cleaned out coconut trees. You could see where your mortar round hit and locate an enemy sniper easily when the top of trees were gone. This was a lot different than the situation in the Solomons and Bairoko, where the trees and jungle were really thick. The mortar men could not even see where their rounds landed in order to adjust their sights. When we got over the cleared beach area, we approached the small rise near Mt. Alifan. We got orders to start digging in and prepare for possible enemy counter-attack. Our Fox Company dug in right above the rise near the waterhole for the animals in the area. N Company and O Company were on either side of us. We were overlooking the landing beach and watching Headquarters Company, and ammo supplies come in before dark. We got dug in before nightfall, and we were getting dug in deep. We piled up the excavated dirt around the hole, which gave us better protection. In the middle of the night, the Japanese tanks came down the road from Mt. Alifan. The marine tanks came in from the area of Agat and met the Jap tanks head on. Through the night, the marine tanks dueled with the Japanese tanks. The marine tanks took charge and virtually wiped out all of the Jap tanks. They were fighting toward each other with close-in cannon fire. As fast as the Jap tanks would come down the mountain road, the marine tanks would blow them to pieces. There was no Japanese coming down the road with the tanks as they were waiting farther up the mountain getting ready for their attack. They were getting buzzed up on saki and beer and getting their courage ready for a banzai attack. We couldn't get any sleep while all the tank fight was going on. The marine tanks did their job—with an excellent outcome. General Patton would have been proud of them. They returned to their area near Agat and watched over the Headquarters Company and the 21st Marines on the rise above the beach. We had star shells and mortars going off as well to watch over us.

The calm was broken by the shouting of "Maline, you die. Maline you die!" They were making all different kinds of noises. "Maline, you die! Maline you die!"

They were yelling and dropping a few grenades around the first wave that came in. The three companies on that rise yelled "Fix Bayonets! No grenades, stay in your foxhole if you can!" The marine tanks were alerted and star shells fell over us. Then the Japs came at us yelling and slashing. There must have been 400 or more. I shot my M1 and expended all eight rounds in my magazine as fast as I could pull the trigger. I grabbed another magazine, popped it in the receiver as fast as I could, and then shot eight more rounds. When the last bullet left my rifle, I heard the familiar "bling." I knew I was out of ammo. I could not get another magazine fast enough, and they were right at us. They were jumping over us, over their dead, our dead, and were going on toward headquarters down below our position. By that time, I was out of my foxhole, jabbing and slashing with my bayonet along with others in the same fix. I got into a hand-to-hand fight with a Jap who would have rather fought than jumped over. We were at it for a while, and I got his arm slashed, but not good enough. I stepped backward and tripped over the mound around my foxhole. As I was going down, he jabbed at me and stuck me in my stomach. I fell into my foxhole, and he was going to finish me off, when a marine next to me put his bayonet through the Jap's back. He really saved my life. As the Jap fell on me, I was able to grab my gung-ho knife I had been using to help dig my foxhole and made sure he was done for—a short jab through his neck. I remained in my foxhole, with pressure on my stomach, as I did not know how bad it was. About 200 of the Japs went through our companies on down to the headquarters area. The tank crews, along with the Headquarters Company, and help from O Company, killed all the banzai Japs.

The three companies on the rise started counting noses, but no one would yell for a corpsman. When daylight came, we started lining up the wounded and dead. I had the dead Jap pulled off of me, and I could see how bad I had been wounded. I was lucky, as the stab wound had gone in on a slant and cut into the stomach muscles. The corpsman put in some sulfur powder and a large compress bandage. After removing all of the marines who were killed, we checked the wounded for those that were considered walking-wounded. We had to take off to help a couple companies that were worse off than we were. I chose to go along with the rest of the company, as my squad had been cut down to three men. Private First Class Navarro (Scout), Private First Class McCoy (BAR man), and myself. That first night attack really took its toll on our company. O Company took the worst of it and lost a lot more men than we did. We heard that the Japanese had built pillboxes all along the coast area. We were supposed to head up the coastline and take out all of the pillboxes, as they were loaded with machine guns and were holding up the hole drive. I was able to walk fairly well and was able to keep up. Navarro was in my lead and helped carry some of the BAR ammo. Then it was me and then McCoy. I tightened my ammo belt around my stomach, and it was evening before I got another dose of the sulfur powder on it. The three companies were on the move going up the coastal area. We were able to clear some of the pillboxes on the way and lost a few more good men along the way. We did find a few of them empty, and some had dead Japs in them. I guess a few marines had been there before us. We saw several dead Japanese that had killed themselves in their special ceremony. They did that because the marines were close and thought we would torture them. Somebody had already taken the knife out of his stomach and now had a knife souvenir. My stomach started to bleed, and I felt I needed to have some more sulfur applied. I called down the line to have the corpsman come back and apply some to my cut. Later, some strange corpsman came back to me and ask what I needed. I asked where the other one was, and he reported that he had been wounded in the leg and hip during our last encounter at a pillbox. He applied the sulfur and pinched the cut tight with tape. He said that would have been the proper way to handle it in the first place. I had no more problems with it from then on, and it started healing right away.

It was very slow for the next four or five days, and we got a little more rest, which was needed. Headquarters was moving up closer to our sector and was supposed to be able to use their larger machine guns on our next push. Flame throwers would most likely be supplied, as we were running into their deeper type of pillboxes. I heard from the new corpsman that one of the first lieutenants got killed a day after we had left the area of Mt. Alifan. The lieutenant was helping out another lieutenant, and his company find the exact location of a pillbox giving them problems and using their machine gun very accurately. The lieutenant got a couple volunteers, and the three of them scouted around the jungle to find the exact location. He found the exact location for the other lieutenant and then led the company in the attack on it. The lieutenant got killed while leading the charge on the pillbox. I looked up the information later and found it almost true. He got the Silver Star for his action and saved a lot of men in that action. I found out the name of the lieutenant as well: 1st Lieutenant Julien E. Leonard. My friend. We were in the 4th Marine Raider Battalion together and later with the 21st Marines. He was from Astoria, Oregon, where I had my first marine duty station. Later in life, I received pictures of Lieutenant Leonard from his mother and dad, Mr. and Mrs. E. E. Leonard of Astoria, Oregon. She said their son was killed on July 28, 1944, and the Silver Star was presented to her and her husband at a ceremony at Tongue Point, Astoria, Oregon, for his service to his country. I later met them in Seaside, Oregon on the ocean turn-around, selling salt water candy.

It was heartbreaking hearing about Leonard getting killed in the same area we were in. A lot of good men lost their lives in that part of Guam. We stayed around the area of Agat and Asan. As we were clearing out some building, our squad found two cases a sake unopened. We decided to bury the sake behind a building and come back after we got Guam secured and have a party. Long story short: We came back after the island was secure and found the Seabees had put up a large postal tent on the same spot. Much later, a trip back to our loot revealed that a building had been erected at the same spot. So...no sake party.

The Guam conflict was supposed to be over and secured on August 10, 1944. However, in our patrols for stragglers, a lot of Japs were killed or captured. Our camp was then located in the middle of a large banana orchard with a barbed-wire fence around the camp area. We had a stalk of bananas tied to our tent pole. We had green coconuts under our cots. We had guard duty around the camp base 24/7 as we found that Japanese stragglers would try to come into camp and get food. The captain of each company would furnish guard-duty patrols throughout the island in search of holdout Japanese. These patrols outside the fence area turned out to be hunting training for future campaigns. The next five months consisted of climbing hills, looking for caves, and assaulting caves. I found that one of the nice things about the long layover was going out for dining on the island. A lot of us would hitch a ride to a place that was nearer the coast than we were located. It was cooler and did have some native food available.

Some of the marines had made friends with the local French families that owned the banana and coconut farms and had been invited to dine with them. My favorite place to dine was with the Seabees at their camp. We were invited to their camp for breakfast, lunch, or dinner. Just bring your own mess gear and wash it before you leave. Boy, those guys really know how to camp and cook. They usually had first choice of all of the food, wine, and liquor that came on the island, as they were in charge of the off-loading. A case of eggs, or maybe a case of officer wine, could come up missing as it came off the supply ship. We were advised to be very selective in eating some of the native food. Just look at some of the natives' teeth and see what Beadle Nut does to them—black. Too much green coconut water/ juice will give you the runs, and too much coconut meat will stop you up. And if you find a Japanese hold out food from a vegetable garden in the jungle near a stream, *do not eat or bring it back to camp.* They fertilize the garden with their own human waste.

1945

We got the word on about February 10, 1945 that we would be moving out soon, "So pack your sea bag and leave it by your sack. Take only what you would need on a daily basis and pack it tight in your back pack. You will get your sea bag after our mission is over and settled in your new encampment." It looked as if our vacation in Guam was over.

Bright and early on February 11th, 1945 we were trucked— yes trucked, not hiked—to our destination on the coast docks. The docks were being loaded with all kinds of equipment, tanks, large mortars, and medical supplies. The 21st Marines of the 3rd Division were being embarked on the U.S.S. President Jackson. As we boarded the ship, we were led directly below deck to our quarters. Instructions were to stay below until we were piped for chow, then return to our quarters—stay below deck. We were unable to see where the balance of the division was loaded as we came aboard. The 21st Marines were to board this ship with some of the 26th Marines. We knew the harbor was very busy getting things prepared for a combat mission. That evening we were allowed to go above deck, and we saw that most of the activity was now in another area. Our ship looked as though they had us all tucked in. It was uncomfortable in our quarters that evening, and sleep was hard to come by. We wanted to know where we were going and when we were going. Smoking light was out, talk was low. I played a few old memory songs on my harmonica. Some guy said,

"Hey, maybe they are taking us home." Another answered, "The Gunny said they are loading too many stretchers for that." I was tired, so I played Taps on my harmonica, and most of the guys figured that that was it for that night. After chow the next morning, we were ordered topside for a meeting and a little exercise. We got introduced to our ship as the U.S.S. Jackson, where the head (toilets) were, and what side of the ship to take if you got sea sick, and were told to stay out of the way of the ship's crew. "Remember, this is their home and have lots of duty to pull with all of their company aboard. Our orders were delayed to sail so we may be at the dock for a while." We were told we would be informed to where we are going as soon as we weighed anchor. So again, this was a "hurry up, and wait" situation.

Two days later, we heard the anchor being pulled out of the water and whistles blowing all over the place. This brought most of the guys out of their bunks and topside to see what was happening. We sailed out of the harbor about one mile and dropped the anchor again. The marines were all ordered to the forward deck of the ship and they handed a small map to each one of us (I still have it). We were told the map was of our main objective: Iwo Jima. That tall thing on the end of the island was Mt. Suribachi, a volcano.

"That is the objective of the 5th Division. The 4th Division will be deployed to the base of that mountain, giving them support from their rear and dividing the island in two parts. The 21st Marines of the 3rd Division will be the floating reserve in the harbor, and if needed, will assist either of the two divisions. The remainder of the 3rd Division will be the reserve force after Mt. Suribachi is secured. This is a small, one-mile by two-mile island with three unfinished airfields being constructed. This island has been held by the Japanese for over twenty years, and we expect a lot of caves, and it has a sandy beach. The island and the airfields have been bombed for about nineteen days and shows considerable damage to both. The Japanese had shipped out Sulphur sand from the quarry at a landing zone. This island is 700 miles north of Guam and 650 south of Tokyo. It is

3,360 miles from Pearl Harbor. I figured that the Japanese had to sail 4,010 miles to bomb Pearl Harbor. You will have cold weather at night, as it is the most North you have been in combat: be prepared."

Most of the good intelligence was gathered in early December, 1944. The navy snooped a submarine, the Spearfish, off the beaches of Iwo Jima. The commander of the submarine watched the activities of the enemy troops and took pictures of the landing area. The defenses of the area seemed to be machine gun, mortars, and antitank guns with the light artillery that had flanking fire along the beaches. They pointed out that the type of sand on the beaches might be difficult for wheeled vehicles. In spite of all the efforts to keep our operation a secret, the Japanese had a fair idea of when the attack would be made and what units would be used. On December 22, 1944, it was alleged that a newspaper printed an article indicating the island target was Iwo Jima, and an American counter-intelligence leaked out a story that is was going to be either Iwo Jima or Okinawa. The Japanese did not buy this leak. In doing some research for dates and names, I found an intelligence report stating that a notebook was found on the body of a dead Japanese with the following information:

"The taskforce will take four days to arrive at Iwo Jima from Saipan. One battleship, eighteen cruisers and destroyers, forty transports left Hawaii. (? and the 5th Marine Division) 3rd and 4th Marine Division, one brigade." I guess rumors came from both sides of the Battle of Iwo Jima.

Now that we had seen and heard our objective, I was trying to figure out just where and when the 21st would be involved. Most of us were more silent than usual and were alone with our own thoughts. We saw more activity around the docks and harbor and guessed it might be the rest of our 3rd Division. I had heard that the 4th and 5th Division were on the 'Canal or Hawaii, so they must have headed toward Iwo Jima already, as they were going to lead the assault. On their way to Iwo Jima, they would stop at Saipan for more supplies.

Finally, on 16 February 1945, we pulled anchor and sailed toward Iwo Jima. The 21st Marines had been aboard the U.S.S. President Jackson for five days just waiting, thinking, praying, and playing poker. The rest of the 3rd Division were to leave the following day.

On February 17, 1945, preparation for the underwater demolition team was to head for the beach, and they would receive covering support from the Cruisers. At 0840 the Nevada, Idaho, and the Tennessee moved in to 3,000 yards from shore, as the demolition team operation was to begin at 1100. However, at 0848 the Tennessee was hit from the Japanese shore batteries, and about one hour later the cruiser Pensacola had several direct hits from the large guns the Japanese had hidden in the mountain caves. The Pensacola then suffered extensive damage and 115 casualties. Among the seventeen that was killed was the executive officer. Included in the large damage the Pensacola received was the observation plane, three crew compartments that flooded, the combat information center that was rendered inoperative, the catapult damaged, a five-inch gun out of action, and the sickbay that was flooded. The ship had received six enemy shells. The UDT (Underwater Demolition Team) swimmers headed toward the beach at about 10.45. The LCI (G's) covered their approach at about 1,000 yards, shooting rocket barrages and 40 mm gunfire. These swimmers were supposed to clear underwater obstacles and destroy them. One swimmer snuck out on the beach and collected soil and sand samples. At about 1100, the LCI's (G) received extremely heavy gunfire from the enemy mortars and large-caliber fixed artillery. The gunboat crew began to answer with their own light armament until they had to retire because of heavy casualties. Nine of the twelve gunboats were put out of action. Due to this action, the crew of the gunboats suffered 132 wounded and 38 killed. The old Nevada, which was close by, answered these larger-caliber guns with their powerful fourteen-inch rifles for almost two hours. The Tennessee, Nevada, and Idaho quickly put down on the entire eastern beach area. The destroyers gave covering for the UDT's and stricken LCI (G's). By 1220, all members of the team were recovered and back aboard transport-destroyers (APD)

I woke up quickly when I heard the, "Now hear this, now hear this. Hit the deck." It was D-Day, February 19, 1945, and the marines were about to arrive on Iwo Jima. The 21st Marines were about nineteen miles from the landing site, and the 4th and 5th Marine Divisions were heading ashore to do battle with the Japanese. The captain of the Jackson had a combat reporter announcing the progress of the Higgins Boats as they approached the landing zone. It had been raining, and rough sea waves were pouncing over the bow of their boat. A few of the marines were sick on his boat. Some from being scared, and some from the tossing of the boat. The beach was quiet; no firing of mortars, no small fire from Jap solders, The American cruisers and battleship had to lift their range, and their shells were landing on the first airfield to give the landing marines safe passage ashore. The 4th and 5th Divisions were landing first and headed fast toward their objective, the mountain. They were to cut across the island. Then the 5th Division would turn left and head up the mountain while the 4th Division would continue forward and cover the base of the mountain.

All of the 21st Marines aboard the Jackson were applauding as we, and maybe other units, thought the Japs had gone—no opposition at all. This was going to be a good dry landing. Then, as our ship got closer to the position of our landing site, it seemed the Devil had opened his gates and let out all the fireworks. The Japs had our troops in a crossfire from Mt. Suribachi and the hills 362 and 382 off of Airfield #2. Higgins boats were exploding, tanks were digging in and not moving, and marines were digging in for cover as deep as they could. The beach was crawling with marines looking for cover. Dead marines littered the landing site. The beach was becoming a junkyard, with all the boats and heavy equipment spread over the whole landing zone. Advancing was almost impossible. The 5th Division got in close to the mountain and hunkered down beneath the boulders and shell holes, then advanced up a little at a time. The ships were firing on the mountain above the marines giving them cover. Rocket ships came in close to the mountain and fired almost point blank as the Japs crawled back into their caves. Flame throwers and hand grenades were the weapon of choice going up, up, up, into the caves and shell holes. The 4th Division had made it across the #3 Airfield and cut over to the other side and base of the mountain. The wounded from the 4th and 5th were coming in to the aid station. The Beach Master had set aside an aid station area that was almost protected from mortar fire.

Rifles were jamming from the volcanic sand and wheeled vehicles were stuck and bored deeper as they rocked back and forth. The marines would dig into the sand for a deeper cover, and the sand would pour back into the hole. The wounded and dead piled up. As darkness came over the landing site, and things calmed down. A few artillery shells and star shells fell around the wounded; small boats and LCV's were attempting to transport them to the hospital ships in the harbor. There were two hospital ships in the harbor waiting for the wounded where they could receive surgery and treatment: The Solace and Samaritan and one Auxiliary Personnel Hospital (APX), the Pinkney. Also assigned for the medical operation was the landing ship vehicle Ozark that would serve as a hospital ship as well. One other hospital ship, the Bountiful, was later scheduled for Iwo duty. In addition, four hospital LST's were to be stationed 2,000 yards off the beaches to serve as evacuation control centers. They would receive the wounded, log them in, give them emergency treatment, and transfer them to other ships for further care. From our ship, we could see the light from star shells that the beach was still covered with dead, wounded, and equipment. The count of the wounded on D- Day was 1,755.

The 21st Marines and the 26th Marines were ordered to prepare to debark and join the attack on Iwo Jima. On February 20, 1945, D plus 1, I was going overboard and into one of the Higgins boats. I was very excited and scared at the possibility of being one of the many dead or wounded on the beach. I did not have any problems crawling down the cargo net. The first over the side and into the boat had pulled the net away from the ship, and it was easier to make the descent. It took about forty-five minutes to get everyone settled in as we formed units around the ship. We circled the Jackson two-by-two. We were ready to turn in to the beach but got the word to hold steady. We held steady and then the Beach Master said they could not take us all — no room on the beach. We circled the Jackson for six hours, bouncing and getting wet from the light rain. We were ordered back aboard our ship by the Beach Master and our commander. I think some of the 26th Division did not get the word or had problems and went in regardless. We followed orders and returned to our ship. I thought to myself, "We die another day."

After getting aboard and being ushered to our bunk, I looked through my pack for dry socks. I don't like wet socks and wet feet. You can get dry rot quickly and get infected, and it is very painful walking on them. I got in line where they were handing out sandwiches and filled my canteen cup with coffee. Sandwiches? Bread with three slices of horse cock (marine slang for baloney) stacked over something called mayo. But with the coffee, they tasted good. A little rest on our bunk, and we listened to orders for the following day.

Early on the morning of February 21, 1945, D-plus 2, the orders came for us to debark from the Jackson. Most of the 21st were already for the call, as they had coffee at the mess hall and had gotten the "straight scoop" from the navy. We got our gear and headed for topside. Naturally, it started to rain, and the wind was getting heavy to morning. We started the routine again with the landing net into the Higgins boat. The boat would be going up and down with the waves, rolling against the ship with each wave of the ocean. If you did not plan the descent, you could get your legs caught between the ship and LCI boat. Those marines that were already in the boat would pull the net away from the ship to counter that effect.

I got ashore, wet and scared from all the mortars landing near our boat. My squad was scattered on both sides of the boat. We were getting machine-gun fire from the quarry walls. Our boat pulled back into the ocean and gave the Jap machine gun a clear shot on those on the left side of the boat. One of my squad members got both legs wounded. He was close to the corpsman for the company. He was patched up and was told to stay in the shell hole and that he would be picked up later. I was short one of my squad now. After the machine gunner was eliminated, we were able to go over the quarry wall and use that position as shelter until those damn mortar men were killed. We were able to regroup and organize the different units of the company to prepare for an advancement toward Airfield #2. We formed a line of riflemen and machine gunners with our mortar men behind us. We could see a large group of Japs between Airfield #2 and our position near the quarry landing. We were supposed to meet the 23rd Marines of the 4th Division at the main landing strip of Airfield #2 between 1000 and 1030 on the 21s of February. We were not going to make that time for sure.

The group of Japs we were now bucking heads with had outflanked the 4th Division that was waiting for us. Those Japs ran into us on the beach area and spoiled their flanking maneuver. We opened fire and stopped them before they got behind the 4th. We could see the Japs getting down in behind trees and brush. We would locate their position and advise the mortar crew. They would fire over our head into the wooded area. By then, our tanks had made it to shore, headed straight into that brush, and covered them up as they fired. We were able to meet up with the 4th at #2 in the morning of the 23rd of February. We started our relief forward, and the 23rd Marines fell back behind us. They really needed that rest, as they had been fighting almost steadily since the first landing on the 19th. This was a hard move, as we were also going over into the 26th Marines zone of action of the 5th Division. The 26th, 23rd, and the 21st were all together on the charge. After we relieved the 23rd, they were still being engaged, and the Japs did their best to continue their fight with them. Our tanks had moved in behind us and began to thrust toward Airfield #2 to help the 23rd Marines.

All during this penetration of our 21st Marines we could hear the ships blowing their horns and making all kinds of noise. I borrowed my scout's binoculars and spotted our flag on top of Mt. Suribachi. The 5th Division had reached the top and placed Old Glory up there, and the ships responded. This was five days after the initial landing of February 19th, 1945.

Our Fox Company of the 21st Marines really got into deep pockets of the enemy. They came at us on a military charge, not like the banzai charge on Guam, but with a coordinated military thrust: mortars, machine guns, anti-tank artillery, hand grenades, and the works. I had been in the banzai attack on Guam and ran out of ammo and received that stomach wound, so I was very careful this time by keeping my spare M1-rifle magazine handier. Then I got hit in the head with a bullet or shrapnel. I was out like a light for about five minutes. A marine from the 23rd saw me move and pulled me to my feet. He said the 21st was in front of him, and he helped me along. I grabbed a helmet from a dead Marine—mine was ruined—and followed him. We traveled another two-hundred yards, picking off Japs that had been passed up. I came in contact with the 21st Fox Company; I found my squad. There were only three of us left now. Me, Private First Class Navarro, and Private First Class McCoy. That charge had cost us a lot of men. I found out later that we had gone through the largest Japanese force on the island. Very little ground was gained that day.

General Schmidt, commander of the whole invasion force, came ashore on the 23rd of February to confer with all of the division commanders. It was decided that the navy and the marine tank divisions would make an assault in the 21st Marines zone of action the first thing in the morning of the 24th of February. The rest of General Erskine's 3rd Division, minus the 21st Marines (as they had already been committed earlier), would land on the 24th of February, with the objective to gain control of the northern plateau, which overlooked the many ridgelines leading to the sea.

On the morning of the 24th of February, the enemy was subjected to a seventy-six minute naval bombardment, a pounding from marine artillery, and a carrier air strike in the 21st Marine zone of action. At 0915, tanks from the 5th Division sector crossed into the 21st sector and attacked the western operation of the airfield. They found that that area was heavily mined and had to withdraw. The enemy had holed up in the hills just north of the airfield. We all fought a bitter fight, going from cave to cave, shell hole to shell hole. We hunkered down that evening and set our foxholes in alternate direction. We had been in the sulfur mines once and knew what the problems were when trying to rest. They smelled like burnt matches and rotten eggs all night. This night would be a little different, as we had a full view of the terrain from all sides of the air strip

The 3rd Division's 9th Marines passed through us on the 25th of February, and at 0930, the division attack got underway. Flame-throwing tanks incinerated the enemy in their shell-proof tunnels. Two days of fighting on that part of the airfield cost our company a lot of men. On the 27th of February, the 9th Marines finally got control of the twin hills just north of us. Then the 21st Marines overran the ruins of Moto Yama Village and seized the hills that dominated Airfield Number 3. After we had gained control of the smaller, Hill 362B, which was overlooking Airfield #3, we were ordered to search the area around the caves to ensure all was cleared. We were to help the 4th Division with Hill 382.

On the last day of February, the 4th Marine Division was still struggling desperately to take Hill 382, which was on the right side. The 5th Division was backed by the Japs on Hill 362A. These hills were the strongest chain of defenses the island had. They were all honeycombed with caves all around the area to give the defenders protection from the artillery and a better view of the approaching invaders. Finally, on the 1st of March, the

28th Marines with the 3d Battalion, made their assault on Hill 362A. At day's end, the American forces had taken Hill 362A. The cost in lives was high: 224 killed and wounded. The objective was to be taken and could not be bypassed.

The 4th Marine Division was still trying to gain a foothold on Hill 382. My squad got mixed up with the 4th Division when their commander commandeered all smaller units when the 21st Marines were passing through Airfield #2. At least I think that is how we ended up going over to the 4th Division. I also heard that Iwo Jima was the first time the divisions worked together under the command of other commanders. Some of the 21st Marines of the 3rd Division were working side by side with the 4th Division.

My squad was trying to attack Hill 382 with the rest of the Company Fox on March 2nd, and again we had to withdraw. We made the attempt two times that day, and the hand grenades and machine-gun fire kept coming from the caves and shell holes at the top. We finally withdrew for the second time that day. The spotters and lookouts for the company located most of where the defenders' fire was coming from. They called for a navy artillery attack the first thing in the morning of March 3rd. Then, just before dawn on the 3rd, the artillery ceased, and we began our attack again. My scout, Private First Class Navarro, went up over the hill, paused, and took a good look-see. My BARman, "Speed" McCoy went over the hill, paused, and took a good look-see. I followed them, and the company corpsman followed me. The Japanese machine gunner on my right opened up with his 25-caliber Nambu He let the first two men go past his cave and put me in his sights. He sprayed me with his first two shots and got me in the right chest, through my chest, chipping my clavicle and lung. It exited my left chest and destroyed my muscle in my upper left arm. I went down and fell into the shell hole near the top. The corpsman jump into the same shell hole unharmed. McCoy turned toward the cave and sprayed the cave and killed two Japs. He and Navarro then jumped behind a large boulder just off the left side of the cave and threw grenades into the cave. The corpsman pulled me back down the hill into a shell hole. The shell hole held several other marines that had been wounded. The corpsman put sulfur (I think) on my right chest and left arm, bandaged them, and went on to the next victim. He tagged me on my blouse with what he had done. Then McCoy came staggering in. He had been hit with a hand grenade and had about one-hundred pieces of shrapnel all over his back. There was not much the corpsman could do, so he tagged McCoy and told us to wait for the stretcher guys. His back was covered with blood spots. He told me about getting the Jap and his helper that shot me. He said the grenade that they threw into the cave must have destroyed many more, as they heard lots of yelling. We stayed in the shell hole a long time waiting for some stretcher bearers to get us. I got a shot of something and some morphine in my arm. They treated McCoy, and we sat hunkered down because the mortars were getting a little too close. Finally, McCoy suggested to give it a try and walk back to the aid beach. He asked if I was up for it, if I could hang on his arm. We waited for the next folly of incoming mortars, then we headed out for the aid station. We figured it to be about a mile if we went straight back alongside the ridge. McCoy left his BAR for some of the other guys. We

left in the shell hole, then he took my M1 for our protection. I grabbed his arm, and we took off. We kept low and just under the ridge. We saw a B-29 circling to land on either Airfield #1 or #2. I think a lot of Japs saw it as well because it brought out a lot firing from caves that had been by-passed. The tanks that had been left in that area took good care of them, and the firing ceased. We were lucky and did not run into any live Japs on the way to the aid station. However, we did see a lot of dead, both American and Japanese.

As we approached the aid station, several corpsmen ran over to meet us and directed us to the correct area. A cameraman was there taking pictures of marines coming in from the front. Boy, we must have made a great picture for him, as we had been bleeding a lot on the way back to the aid station. I was laid on a stretcher, back-side down. McCoy was laid on a stretcher, back-side up. As I was being put down on the stretcher, I felt wet and a sharp pain in my left chest. I felt under my shirt on my left side, and my finger went into a big hole in my left chest. I told the corpsman he better look there, as I had another hole in my chest that the first corpsman did not find. He then applied some medication to that and bandaged it with fresh bandages and searched for more holes around my chest area. The feeling of pain was beginning to come back from the three holes now. Some from actual pain, and the rest from being scared finding those holes that close to my heart.

We were side by side seeing all of the first arrivals get loaded on to LST's that were ferrying them to the hospital ships in the harbor. The beach was littered with sunken LCI's, LCT's, Tanks and all kinds of wheeled vehicles. It wasn't very long before a couple of LST's dropped anchor and then roared up the beach. Two guys grabbed my stretcher and put me aboard in the stern of the boat. All of the stretcher cases went in the stern side by side. The ambulatory wounded came aboard by themselves and kneeled down to keep out of the line of fire. That was a very bumpy ride back through the turf to get away from all those sunken boats that had not made it to the beach. I did not see McCoy anymore after he walked into the boat. I am glad I had a chance to visit with him, share a cigarette, and thank him for all our memories fighting through Guam and Iwo together. I think I would have lost my life had I not had his help leaving that shell hole on Hill 382. He told me that Navarro had been just in front him when he got hit with the grenade; however, he didn't think Navarro went down at the time. So neither one of us knew what happened to him after we got hit. I think maybe he was the only one left in our squad from that encounter on Hill 382. I heard later that most of our Fox Company had lost their lives or were wounded making that last charge before it was finally secured.

Our boat pulled up to the gang plank of the hospital ship Solace. The ambulatory wounded were helped off the boat and up the gang plank. The wounded that were still on stretchers were lifted onto the deck of the hospital ship by crane. The stretchers were then picked up by several sailors and taken to the medical surgical area. I guess I must have blacked out from pain by then. When I came to, the two doctors were discussing my condition, and it didn't sound good. The younger of the two physician said he had probed the entry and could not find any foreign body at that time; there were exit holes on my left chest with loose skin gathered in and around the holes, and there were some bone fragments and lots of muscle tissue as well. He said they would have to remove the torn muscle and look for loose bone. By that time, I was getting very interested in their conversation about my condition. He then looked at my left arm, raised my forearm, and it fell down on the gurney. After several attempts to find life in the arm, and a very weak pulse, if any, at the wrist, the two doctors just looked at each other. The muscle area was torn and bleeding in several places. The older doctor indicated that they would most likely have to remove the arm just above the muscle. When I heard that I really came wide-eyed and alive. The younger doctor seem to agree and indicated they would do that first. Now I had heard about surgeons doing unnecessary surgery on arms and legs in Guam and other combat campaigns. This seem to be the faster method to save time. It was easier to cut-off than to sew up tendons, blood vessels, and other necessary things that make the limbs work correctly. Also, maybe their medical training had not included this level of surgery. Anyway, I objected to their decision loudly and indicated I did not want my arm removed. The young doctor said I would have a lot better use from a prosthetic arm than one just dangling from the shoulder. As he reached for something from the surgical tray, I threw a hay-maker at him with my right hand. The needle in my right hand pulled out and pulled down the thing on which it was attached. I hit the doctor on the right chin and shoulder, and he hit the surgical tray and it went flying. Two assistants grabbed me and held me down. Words flew from me, the doctors, and the assistants. I told the doctors I was sorry to have expressed my feelings so strongly and was very sorry. After we all calmed down, the doctors agreed not to cut off anything and repair what they could and see what the results were. I was given a shot of something, and I went out like a light within a few seconds. I woke up later in a large room where there were about fifteen other post-surgical military personnel. I saw that I still had both arms and still could not move the left arm. My chest was all bandaged nicely as well. I had thought I had really crapped in my own mess gear for acting like I did and before they had even started on the other things. My left arm was in a sling and the left and right side of my chest really hurt from where they must had been probing for foreign stuff. Later, I was able to review the chart hanging at the foot of my bed to review what they were doing to me now and what the diagnose was. I surprised when it read "COMBAT FATIGUE." I had expected it to read "GSW, Left arm and chest." I guess they thought my response in the surgery room put me in another status. The note that the doctor used in his diagnosis followed me throughout my entire medical stay aboard ships and in hospitals.

I got some needed sleep, as I had not had any good solid sleep for the previous twelve days on Iwo. I fought each battle I was in over and over. My stomach was empty, my bladder was full, and I hadn't had but one good bowel movement in those twelve days, and my colon was yelling, "Help!" That "good one" happened right after the big fight on Air Field #2 when we stopped at the Sulfur Mines and dug in for the night. I think the fumes helped solve the problem.

(My Mother and Father received a notice from the Casualty Branch of the Adjutant General War Department on March 12, 1945 that I had received "gunshot wounds of my left chest" in action and was "making normal improvement.")

•   •   •   •   •

We arrived in Saipan about ten days later, on March 17, 1945, and we were off-loaded to the USAGH #148 on the island. They looked at my tag and put me in the area that was taking care of that kind of problem. When I got assigned to a certain area and bedded down and things got a little quiet, I asked one of the corpsman to take care of my bandages. They had not been looked at or changed for four or five days, and I was getting a little "rank," and the pain was worse. He said he would get to it a little later. I had to ask another corpsman to take care of those wounds, as they were bothering me. Finally, one looked at my tag and told me I was in the wrong area and to get changed. I was transferred into another ward. The doctors were upset about the condition of the wounds and the area that I had been billeted. I was taken into the operative room and removed all the bandages and the left arm sling. He advised the nurses to start physical therapy on the left arm, as it had a strong pulse and was getting color back into it. He listened to my chest and then told the nurses to make an appointment for the surgical room the next day to perform a TAP. After the exam was over, I asked the nurse "What is a TAP?" She said that a blood vessel was loose in my left chest, and I was bleeding inside my chest cavity. He was going to insert a long needle into the chest area or back and drain all the blood gathered inside. That mostly was the reason I was having pain in that location. Now that didn't sound too good to me. I was removed from the operating room and put back into my bed.

I went to sleep right away, thinking about the morning procedure and what they planned to do. I guess I moved around a lot in bed, as I still had some of the battles being fought in my head. I woke up, and it felt like I was sweating and lying in a pool of water. I called out to the night nurse to change my bedding. She turned the night light on, turned it off right away, and left. She and two more nurses came back with the doctor. I had moved around a lot in bed and turned over on my left side, and blood came pouring out the hole in my chest. I was lying in a pool of blood—not water. The doctor said to hold me in the left side position until all the loose blood was out of the chest. They clamped the blood vessel and moved me back into the operative room to clean me up, stitched the blood vessel well, and stitched the hole closed. He told the nurses to cancel the appointment for the TAP process, as I had done the emptying of the chest cavity already. Now that was good news to me.

(On March 25, 1945, my mother and father received a notice from Major D. Routh, USMC Casualty Headquarters Washington, reporting that I had been wounded on March 3, 1945 on Iwo Jima, Volcano Islands.)

• • • • •

On March 31, 1945, I was traveling again. This time I was to be flown to Pearl by a PBY-3 plane with twenty other marines. We were in a bunk space that was rigged to hold stretchers. After moving out into the harbor, the plane started the takeoff. We really bounced around during this time, as the waves were rough that morning. Speaking of waves...there were two really nice-looking army nurses aboard the plane taking care of us. Now that was medicine any marine could use...TLC.

Several hours later, we landed on the ocean just off Johnson Island. This was a little north of Pearl Harbor and nothing but a fuel stop. We pulled up to a dock, and an army man came aboard with a spray tank.

He walked up and down the aisle spraying us with God knows what. We were notified that we had been in the tropics and may have picked up some foreign bugs that could be transferred over to the main island. Heaven forbid that we would cause bugs to get on the main island, foreign or otherwise.

After the plane and its cargo had been sanitized, the plane took off again to Pearl Harbor. On March 31, 1945, we landed in the bay and were met with several medical boats. They brought us ashore, looked at our medical tag, and assigned each of us the proper ward according to our diagnose. After I settled down, I asked the duty nurse to look after my bandages, as I thought they needed changed. She got in touch with her head nurse, and they both removed the bandages and applied a new one on my arm and left chest. The hole on my right chest was doing fine. A note on my left arm sleeve suggested to have my arm massaged at least once a day. The duty nurse said she would take care of that a little later. When she returned, I told her of the ordeal aboard ship about them wanting to cut my arm off. She understood why they wanted to have my arm massaged and said she would take care of it as long as I was stationed there in the hospital. I was in the hospital on Pearl for about a week, so I did not get much sightseeing around the island. I received good care, as I got pain medication most anytime I wanted. I had periods of forgetfulness and even missed several meals, they said.

I left Pearl with several other marines on April 8th, 1945. We were shipped out aboard the U.S.S. Admiral R.E. Coontz on the way to San Francisco, California. I still had a tag on my baggage saying combat fatigue, but someone was going to change it to W.I.A. (Wounded In Action) and post it on the medial chart. However, I ended up in the "Ward #13," or the "Nut Ward," as we called it. We landed in San Francisco, California aboard ship, and was there two days left on April 10th, 1945. Now, how I got to San Diego, California, I do not remember. Maybe it was a San Francisco stop over, staying several days putting others on board to take to San Diego. I know that is where I ended up after I was wounded on Iwo Jima. I had been over in the Pacific Theater fighting against the Japanese for two years, twenty-six days—over 50 percent of my four-year enlistment.

(On April 17, 1945, my mother and father received a notice from M. C. Craig, First Lieutenant, USMC Washington, D.C., that I had received gunshot wounds of the chest and was making normal improvements).

· · · · ·

On April 12, 1945, I had an appointment with the shrink (doctor) to see if I could be released and assigned to the duty station of my choice. While waiting in the waiting room and listening to the radio, a breaking announcement came over the news: The President of the United States, my Commander in Chief, had just died of a stroke. Boy, what news that was. I was just about ready to see the doctor when the news came on. I was being questioned by the doctor and making conversation, and I mentioned that the president had just died, and a guy by the name of Truman was now the president. The doctor thought I was nuts and called in his doctor friend from the next room. He looked at my chart and said, "No kidding." Well from that little talk, they both thought I was nuts, and I was not released and stayed in for another week or so.

I was still in "Ward #13," classified as combat fatigue, which is now classified as PTSD. Maybe the doctors saw something about me, my appearance, or my attitude that gave them the idea that I was in the correct ward. I probably did some crazy things that gave them these ideas. Like when I would go to chow, I would break into the front of the line. Or when the navy needed another barber, I said I was one because I used to cut the hair of my squad when overseas. Or when my girlfriend (Katherine Salmon) called me and said she was coming to California to visit me in the hospital, I went AWOL for a weekend by removing my clothes, tying them on my head and wading and swimming the mote around the hospital to go visit her. After all, she was the girl I had met in Astoria, Oregon; my first date, the fifteen-year-old high school girl (now seventeen), the one I had been writing to for the last two years. She was now going to be a senior in high school and had to get permission from the principal to make the trip. I could not get liberty at that time, so I just "jumped ship" for the weekend. It happened that her married sister, Bernice, lived in San Diego, and she was going to stay with them. I returned to the hospital that Sunday evening, repeated my swim, and got into my ward without being missed. After all, there were only nutcases in that ward.

I was asked what duty station I would like to serve to end my four-year enlistment. I wasn't sure, but I did want to be near my parents. I had not seen them since my enlistment over three year before. They said that with my experience in the Marine Raiders and in combat duty in four major campaigns in the Pacific, I would be a good drill instructor on combat training. Paris Island was the closest station to my hometown. So the ball started rolling in motion to get me transferred out of the hospital.

On July 19, 1945, I was transferred to Casualty Headquarters Camp Pendleton but did not have to report to Parris Island, South Carolina until August 19th, 1945. I was transferred but did not have to report there for thirty days. A thirty-day furlough transfer was given to me because I had just gotten back from overseas.

I caught a train in San Diego and headed to Portland, Oregon with my destination to see my girlfriend in Astoria. I wanted to spend part of my leave with her and ask her a few questions. I had not seen her for three years and wanted to make sure she felt the same way about me as I did about her. The train went by my old duty station, Tongue Point, on the way into Astoria. The shades were pulled down on the train, so I was unable to see the main gate of the facility. She met me at the depot, and when I saw her, my heart skipped a beat. She was really in that skipped beat.

Two of Katherine's girlfriends were renting a one-bedroom apartment in Astoria, and the plan was to go there and stay for the night before I headed for Arkansas. The two girls slept in the bedroom, and they had a single cot set up in the kitchen for Katherine. That evening after supper and a visit with the three girls, we decided to retire for the evening. The two girls had to be at work the next day. Katherine and I sat up *all* night talking and getting acquainted. She was a nice girl, and I was a nice boy. We really didn't get anything settled about marriage. She wanted to graduate from high school, and I wanted to get a discharge from the marine corps. Both of these objectives would happen in the next year, 1946.

I stayed with the three girls that evening, and they drove me to the train depot in Astoria the following morning. I got to Portland at about noon and hitched a ride to the Portland Air Military Base. I checked in to the military flight office to see if I could hitch a ride on a military plane to Little Rock, Arkansas. They had nothing going to Arkansas for the next couple days. They had a cargo flight going to Kansas City, Kansas in about two hours, and if I wanted to sit on boxes, I could go as far as Kansas City. I took that free flight and had a good one, courtesy of the U.S. government. After we arrived in Kansas City, one of the military men took me over to the train depot. I made arrangements to take the train going south with a stopover in Little Rock, Arkansas. I had a fun time on that railroad car, as it was really crowded with servicemen.

COMING HOME

As the train pulled in to the station, I spotted my dad waiting for it to stop. He sure looked good to me, as I had not seen him for over three years. After a few good hugs, he took me over to the parking area where mother was waiting. Dad had borrowed a car from one of the ladies in the neighborhood, with the plan to also take her and her daughter with him to meet me. When I saw those people, I could see a set-up right away, but the daughter was just not my type. Mother and I had a nice cry and discussed how different I looked now. When I left home in 1942, I weighed 128 pounds and was 5-foot-6 inches. Now I was 5-foot-9 inches and 160 pounds. I asked where my little brother Charles was and was told that there was not enough room for him in the car. Funny. There was room for a strange woman and strange daughter and not enough room for my brother.

That evening after supper, Dad and Mother, Charles and I had a nice talk about my war experience in the Pacific. It got around to them wanting to see where I had been shot. I told them I still had some bandages on, as I didn't want any stains on my shirt. Mother gasped, Charles said "Gahlee," and Dad was a little ticked off. My left chest had about a half inch of muscle sticking out of the hole. The hole was trying to heal, but the flesh sticking out of it would prevent it from doing so. He said he was going to take me over to the base hospital the next day. Dad was working, and living, at the Pine Bluff, Arkansas Army Arsenal Ammunition facility, which had

their own medical section. He was the assistant manager of the poison gas and ammunition igloos there. He said he wanted the army doctors to look at the wound, as it did not look good to him. Dad had served in WWI over in France and had seen a few things like that.

When we arrived at the hospital the next day, they were able to see me right away. The doctor look at my wounds, and he got really upset also. He said a few bad words about the navy doctors releasing me for duty in that shape. I told him the story about the combat fatigue mix-up I had since the day I slugged the surgeon onboard ship and how they released me from headquarters section and didn't even review the medical records. He had me rolled into the surgery room, gave me a shot in the left chest, and started cutting . He cut all of the muscle tissue off, which he called "Proud Flesh," and said the hole would now begin to heal. This picture of me was taken sitting on my family's porch after being in the army surgery and patched up (August 1945).

Purple Heart Medal Awarded Corporal Frank S. Wright

MARINE CPL. FRANK S. WRIGHT

At a ceremony held recently at the U. S. Naval Hospital, Oceanside, Calif., Marine Corporal Frank Wright, son of Mr. and Mrs. Joseph L. Wright of Plainview, received the Purple Heart Medal for wounds inflicted by enemy action in the Pacific Theater of War.

Chief Warran Officer George A. Royse, commanding officer, casual Detachment, Marine Barracks, Camp Pendleton, read the citation accompanying the medal and Navy Captain I. W. Jacobs, (MC) USN, commanding officer of the hospital made the presentation.

After we got home and everyone reviewed the army's doctor work, we did a lot of family gossip, catching up. They wanted to know a lot about my girlfriend Katherine. Mother thought she was Jewish. She thought her name was Solomon. I told them she was Finnish and her last name was Salmon. Mother wanted me to try to see her brother (my uncle) who lived in Washington, D.C. Also, try to visit my older brother, Joseph, in Florida. He was in the army and stationed in Florida. As a D.I at Parris Island, I could get seventy-two-hour passes often. At least that was what I was told by the master sergeant at the base. Mother said Aunt Janie, her sister, was coming to visit the next week. She was the one that signed my fake delayed birth certificate. I say fake because it had never been officially state certified, and the recruiting sergeant didn't catch it.

I stayed around the arsenal with my family most of the time while on this furlough. I toured the arsenal with Dad, and I saw all the restricted poison gas storage areas, where the shells and grenades were kept, and how they were shipped out by rail and truck. Also, I was shown where the Japanese internment camp was and was told how some of them were given day leaves to go into town. A lot of the people in town objected to them shopping around town for plants and seed for vegetable gardens. The army still had 24/7 guards around the camp.

My time was up on my leave, and I had to catch a train to Parris Island. I was to report on August 19th, 1945 for full duty as a Drill Instructor, Combat Action. My job was to go to different boot camp platoons and tell them things about jungle fighting, close-quarter fighting, knife-fighting, and some about Judo, most of which I had learned when I was in the Marine Raiders. At the time, I was the only Marine Raider that had returned to Parris Island as an instructor. The Marine Raiders were the first ever special forces created by the U.S. Marines. The Corps created four Battalions in 1942. The last of the original Marine Raiders left the United States for the Pacific Theater in February 1943.

I had a 72-hour pass coming up, so I called my Uncle John (my mother's brother) in Washington, D.C. He invited me over to see him and go to one of the football games in Washington. He said he had an honor box at the game and had a few more guests going to the game with him. I accepted and took a bus headed to Washington. The bus station was three blocks from his downtown apartment. He had a car there waiting for me— neat huh? His apartment was really nice. And Aunt Helen was very nice looking. We had a brandy, visited, and went on to the game. The Washington Redskins were playing an out-of-town team, I forgot who. I do remember that the Redskins had a one-armed player playing defense on the line, and he used it really well. We were sitting in box seats on the fifty-yard line. I sat by Uncle John. On his left were two senators, and on my right were two army generals. Uncle John passed me a brandy flask. I took a shot from it, I passed it on to the two generals, and they took a shot as well. For the rest of the game, we were six regular guys.

It seems that Uncle John was a highly important insurance agent in

Washington, and I was their high guest of honor. After the game and visits, my accommodations included a guest room at Uncle John's hotel apartment. I visited with them for a while, and he paid for my bus fare back to my base.

After I had seen most of the young marines in boot camp, I was assigned as an assistant drill instructor. My experience with them, and showing them how to stay alive using their training skills, were some of the most satisfying experiences of my four-year enlistment. The marine corps was my mother and father, teacher, and religious training all through my teenage years. I went into the marines at the age of sixteen and was out at nineteen years of age. I am still a marine, off-duty. As the marines say: "Once a Marine, always a Marine."

AND THE REST OF THE STORY

1946 TO 2018

My four-year enlistment was finished on January 21, 1946. So I expected to leave Parris Island on that date. I went to the marine head office to pick up my discharge papers and was all ready to hitchhike to see my brother Joseph in Florida. CLOSED. The office was closed and would not be open until Monday, January 22nd. So I was to serve four years and one day in the marines.

I got my papers Monday morning and headed for the nearest gate that would afford me the best chance to get a ride. The guards at the gate said I could not leave the boot-camp area, as my cover (hat) was on crooked, my tie was loose, and my belt wasn't shined and neither were my shoes. My metals were not shined, and they were crooked. After giving me a bad time about my uniform, they said I looked great, and they were just kidding. They said, "Give them hell marine, and good luck." They saluted me and said have fun in Florida.

I caught several rides on my way to see my brother in Florida. I had not seen my brother for four years. He and his wife had a small apartment near his army post. I had met his wife before I went into the marine corps. My brother, his wife, and I, used to go roller skating where he was working at the time. He was a skate monitor and skated backwards watching the patrons for problems. He had met his wife there, and they got married before he was drafted into the army.

After I visited with my brother and wife for a while, I wanted to go to town and shop for a set of civilian clothes. I felt like I was really out of the marines when I got into those clothes. Then I wanted a "civilian hat" (cover). Now I was really a civilian, but I had a marine overcoat on, and that looked weird.

After supper and some talk about his thinking of making the army his retirement future, they set up a cot in the kitchen, and I went to sleep right away. I had one of those "bad" dreams and woke up shaking again. That was one thing that followed me all through my life: bad dreams and shakes. In 1946, they called these things post-combat fatigue. Now they refer to it as PTSD.

I took a bus to Little Rock and slept most of the way. I arrived at the bus station, and Dad was there with Mother and Charles. He had borrowed a car from one of his buddies at work. I looked different this time with civilian clothes on. Dad and I talked about me buying a car so I could find a job.

He was using a government car at work, but it was for business use only and on base. His finances were not good, and the money I had been sending home for four years was not around anymore. Now that is a story in itself as to where it went.

I made a loan at a local bank and bought a 1938 Ford car. I got a job as a traveling salesman at H.L. Blake Wholesale Co., as one of my high school buddies was the manager of sales there. I traveled all over southern Arkansas to small-town gas stations with my goods. They are called Mini-Marts now. That is how I was paying for my loan on the car, which needed to be repaired. I needed a car in good condition, as I had planned on a trip to Oregon. I wanted to see my girlfriend. My finances were going downhill fast, with buying a car, gas, repairs, and sleeping on the road. Civilian life was costly.

I had planned on going to Oregon in July, as I would most likely have enough money to make the trip and stay up there for a month. Dad had a friend that wanted to go to California, as his brother got him a job there. He told me he would share the expenses if I would take them (he and his wife) to California on my way to Oregon, and they would share the driving. However, he had to go in June to get the job. I thought that would be a great deal and save a lot. He said we could stop over to a sister's house in Texas on the way.

The trip over to California was not too exciting and was no trouble with the car. We did stop over at the sister's house in Muleshoe, Texas for one night. That afternoon and evening there was a big sand storm, and my little 1938 Ford was not under cover. That night the sand blew so hard, it blew sand through the key hole in the front door and left a trail inside the house about twelve-feet long. My car was loaded with sand, and we had to clean the motor off to get it to run, and the air cleaner was loaded.

We finally arrived in Los Angeles, and I let him off at a bus station to seek transportation to his brother's house. I then started north to Oregon by myself. The ride was okay, but the traffic was busy, even in those days. I got rest where I could find a good place to stop off the road. There were many orange-juice stands along the highway that had enough room to park a car for a short time. The orange-juice stands were in the shape and color of a large plaster orange. There was fresh orange-juice at each one of the stands. I think I got some food as well when I stopped; however, I know I filled up on the juice.

It took about twenty-four hours to get to Katherine's house, and I had directions by mail on how to get there. I had been there once when I was stationed at Tongue Point, so I knew a little about the direction. She was there, as well as her young sister Eileen, and Mom and Pa Salmon.

Our courtship was short, as well as my finances. I wanted to get married right away; she wanted to wait for a while. I told her that if she did not marry me now, on this trip, she most likely would not marry me at all. She said she always wanted to get married in June. Well, we got married on the last day of June: June 30, 1946. Yes, the same little girl who was my first date in 1942. At this writing, we have been married for seventy-two years. I am ninety-three years old, and she is ninety-one years old. I still have problems with bad dreams and shakes, and sometime I yell at night. I still go to PTSD group meetings at the V.A. I have given speeches at the Marine Corps Birthday Celebration, at the Navy Birthday Celebration, at the Fleet Marine Force celebration, at the Iwo Jima Landing celebration, and at the ending of the hostel forces on Iwo Jima. I threw out the first pitch at the Stockton Ports baseball game in celebration of Veterans Day.

I went to Linfield College in McMinnville, Oregon and got educated in accounting and business education. I worked as a bookkeeper in lumber and logging companies. We later moved to California, and I worked as a medical business consultant and then opened my own office in Lodi, California.

Katherine has supported me in all my hobbies and military-veterans activities. I have supported her in all her hobbies and other activities. We are still good friends, and that is what holds a marriage together.

We have raised three boys and have three daughters-in-law, four grandchildren, and eleven great-grandchildren.

Notes

Top: Marine Gung Ho
Center: Marine K=Bar
Bottom: Raider Stiletto

The three knives shown are from my knife collection. They were reproduced as authentic replicas of the real items by The U.S. Marine Raider Foundation

RESOURCES

Commandant of Marine Corp: 1984 Copy of history of Frank S. Wright in U.S.M.C. 1942 - 1946

Ships data of debarkation and arrivals and dates of departures.

Iwo Jima: Legacy of Amphibious Epic, Historical Branch, G-3 Division, Hdq. U.S. Marine Corps

Real Blood, Real Guts: James Gleason

Iwo Jima: Richard F. Newcomb

Iwo Jima, Portrait of a Battle: Eric Hammel

The Marine Raiders: Edwin P. Hoyt

Red Blood, Black Sand: Charles W. Tatum

U.S. Marine Corps Raiders 1942-1946: Ed Gilbert

U.S. Marine Raiders Association: Raider Patch

U.S. Marine Raider Foundation

NOTES

The names of ships and the dates of embarkation and destinations were located in my personal records received from the National Personnel Records Center, 9700 Page St., St. Louis, Missouri. I requested them on 19 September 1984. I also retrieved names and dates from other media.

The picture labeled "Me and 'Speed' McCoy" was located in the book *Red Blood, Black Sand* by Charles W. Tatum. Charles Tatum was in the 27th Marines, 5th Division. He also was on Iwo Jima during the initial invasion and traveled over the same terrain as I did. A picture in his book, page 252, pictures two wounded marines with both of them tagged, one holding the arm of the other, walking toward the beach where the medical evacuation center had gathered. It has no mention of who took it. I am sure it is the picture of me and "Speed" McCoy walking back to the medical area after we had been wounded. I give "Chuck" the credit for finding that picture, and I am sure he would allow me to post it in my book. Chuck and I were in the Stockton Marine Club together, and I have his book, autographed. Tatum went to the Iwo Jima campaign right out of boot camp in 1945.